EPHESIANS:
LESSONS IN GRACE

How To Believe,
Receive And Share
God's Gift Of Grace

ERIC ELDER

DEDICATION

Dedicated to Mary Lou Schrock,
one of the most gracious
women I know.

ACKNOWLEDGMENTS

Special thanks, as always, to my wife, Lana, who read and revised each of these devotionals as I was writing them, infusing them with additional spiritual insights and practical wisdom.

Introduction

THE GRACE OF AN AMERICAN IDOL

Scripture Reading: Ephesians 3:18-19

Even if you've never watched *American Idol*, you may still have heard of Adam Lambert. He competed in the grand finale of this nation's most famous singing contest.

Besides having an astounding voice, there's another thing that stands out to me about this top contender: his consistent graciousness.

When complimented by the judges for an outstanding performance, Adam readily offers his thanks to those in the band who helped make it possible. When asked by the host how he'll be adding his own spin to a famous song, Adam compliments the one who wrote the song, saying that it was so well-written there's little he could add to make it better.

It seems that almost every time a compliment comes his way, Adam steers the praise towards those around him.

While not many of us will ever be able to

sing like Adam Lambert, we can all take a lesson from this other facet of his life that has helped to make him so incredibly successful: his graciousness towards others. Does this mean we should follow his example in everything he does? Of course not! We all do some things that are more honoring to God than others. But his graciousness is something we would all do well to emulate.

When your thoughts, words and actions are filled with grace, people are naturally drawn towards you. They're more likely to listen to what you have to say, to do what you ask them to do, and to become all that they can become. God wants you to be grace-filled, not only because it will enhance *your* life, but because it will enhance the lives of those around you as well.

God knows what a blessing graciousness can be because He's been showering people with grace throughout human history. He knows that the best way to express His love to others is to overwhelm them with His grace.

God's grace has helped transform countless lives, turning some of the most sour, bitter and angry people into people who are the most joy-filled, happy, and delightful people I know. I've also seen how those who don't understand God's grace, or who find it hard to understand or receive, also find it hard to express grace to others in meaningful or practical ways.

As for me, well, I guess I'm somewhere in between! I'd like to be more consistently gracious, but I'm not there yet. Sometimes I'm just too self-focused. Sometimes I become critical of others, forgetting how much grace God has already showered upon me. Sometimes I'm just not thinking, and ungraciousness slips out when I should have been gracious instead. Whatever the reason, I know that I have a lot to learn and a lot of room to grow.

So in the coming weeks, I'm going to be taking a closer look at the book of Ephesians, and I'd be glad for you to take a look along with me. Even though the book is only six chapters long, Ephesians is one of the most grace-filled books in the whole Bible. The Apostle Paul, who wrote the book originally as a letter to the Christians in the ancient Greek city of Ephesus (now modern-day Turkey), filled his letter with grace both in words and tone.

From the opening words to the closing line, Paul uses the word "grace" a dozen times, encouraging the Ephesians to understand and receive God's grace for themselves and then to extend it to others. He prayed for them the same prayer that I'll be praying for you, and for myself, in the weeks ahead:

> "...that you, being rooted and established in love, may have power, together with all the saints, to grasp how wide, and long and high and deep is the love of Christ, and to know this love that surpasses knowledge—that you may be filled to the measure of all the fullness of God" (Ephesians 3:18-19).

I'm looking forward to this study of the book of Ephesians. I pray that God will overwhelm you with His grace, and that you'll find it the most natural thing in the world to pour it out on others as well.

If you've never read the book of Ephesians before, I think you'll find it to be filled with both grand thoughts about God and practical suggestions for your life. For those who have read it before, I think you'll be amazed at how many of the most famous verses in the Bible are found in this very short book.

At the top of each devotional, I've included a Scripture Reading that I encourage you to read on your own, as I don't include the full text of Ephesians in this book. When you're finished reading each of these Scripture Readings, you'll have read through the entire book of Ephesians.

I've also included a prayer at the end of each devotional that you can use to pray along with me. I hope this helps you to begin a quiet time of prayer with God in response to what you've read. To get you started, here's today's prayer:

PRAYER: FATHER, THANK YOU FOR THE GRACIOUSNESS THAT WE'VE SEEN DISPLAYED IN THE LIVES OF OTHERS, AND THANK YOU FOR THE GRACIOUSNESS THAT YOU'VE SHOWERED UPON US. HELP US, LORD, TO BE FILLED SO MUCH WITH YOUR GRACE THAT IT FLOWS OUT TO THOSE AROUND US AS WELL, BLESSING THEM—AND OURSELVES—ALONG THE WAY. IN JESUS' NAME, AMEN.

Lesson 1

GRACE BEGINS
WITH A THOUGHT

Scripture Reading: Ephesians 1:1-2

Some people think that being kind and gracious is a sign of weakness, but the exact opposite is true. The measure of graciousness in your life is the true measure of your strength.

According to the 19th century British hymn-writer, Frederick W. Faber:

> *"Kindness has converted more sinners than zeal, eloquence, or learning."*

Being kind and gracious towards others, even when they give you no reason to be kind to them, can have a greater and longer-lasting impact on their lives than perhaps anything else you could offer them. But where does grace begin? Where can you start if you want to be more gracious in your life? The answer I've found is this: grace begins with a thought.

One of my favorite birthday presents was a bottle of water. What I loved so much about this present wasn't just the water itself, but the thought behind it.

It started years earlier when I was on a business trip to New York. During a meeting, someone at the table asked if I'd like anything to drink. I didn't want to be a bother, and I didn't want them to have to spend anything on me, so I just said, "Sure, I'll take some water."

But a few minutes later, this man came back with a cold bottle of the most incredible water I had ever tasted in my life. I had no idea water could taste so good! It turned out to be a bottle of Evian mineral water, imported from the mountains of France.

When I came back from that trip, I went to the store to see if I could get some more bottles of that water. I went into sticker shock at the price. I decided I didn't need to relive that experience bad enough to pay that much. But I must have mentioned it to my family, because when my birthday came around, my oldest son, who was still pretty young at the time, went out and bought me a few bottles of Evian water.

I asked my wife if she told him to get it for me, but she didn't. He just thought of it himself.

I was touched. It wasn't like I talked or dreamed about this water all the time. But here my son had made a mental note of something that was special to me, and when a special occasion arose, he went out and got it for me. It wasn't an expensive gift as far as gifts go—even though it was expensive as far as water goes! But what made it so special was the thought that went into it.

And that's where grace begins: with a thought.

In the book of Ephesians, the Apostle Paul opens with these words:

"Paul, an apostle of Christ Jesus by the will of God, To the saints in Ephesus, the faithful in Christ Jesus: Grace and peace to you from God our Father and the Lord Jesus Christ" (Ephesians 1:1-2).

Paul wished for them to have God's grace and peace in their lives, and he meant it! He backed up his graceful thoughts towards them by writing the letter. Perhaps the most gracious thing about this whole letter is that Paul took time to write it at all!

Here he was, bound in chains as a prisoner in Rome. But rather than focusing on himself and his own problems, he took the time to send a letter to those who needed some encouragement in their lives. That one act of kindness is still impacting lives today, as we're still reading and learning from the words that Paul took the time to write almost 2,000 years ago!

If you want to grow in graciousness towards others, the best place to start is with a thought. Take some time to let your thoughts roam through different ways you could express grace to those around you. Pick up a pen. Pick up a phone. Pick up a bottle of water.

It doesn't take much to be gracious, but it does take some thought. Give it some thought today. You'll be blessed—and you'll be a blessing—when you do.

PRAYER: FATHER, THANK YOU FOR THE KINDNESS THAT YOU'VE SHOWN TO ME, AND I PRAY THAT YOU'D HELP ME TO SHOW IT TO OTHERS. GIVE ME YOUR THOUGHTS TO KNOW HOW I CAN BE A

BLESSING TO THOSE AROUND ME TODAY. IN JESUS'
NAME, AMEN.

GOD'S GRACE IS GLORIOUS AND LAVISH

Scripture Reading: Ephesians 1:3-23

Have you ever tried to describe something incredible—a beautiful sunset, a magnificent canyon, a massive mountain—but your words seem to fall flat? No matter how hard you try to describe it, you know that the only way others will be able to catch a glimpse of what you're trying to describe is if they can somehow experience it themselves?

It seems that this is what the Apostle Paul may have felt as he tried to describe God's grace in the book of Ephesians. As much as Paul tried to describe it, as both "glorious" and "lavish," Paul knew that the best way for the Ephesians to fully understand what he was saying was for them to experience it themselves. So he prayed:

"I keep asking that the God of our Lord Jesus Christ, the glorious Father, may give you the Spirit

of wisdom and revelation, so that you may know Him better. I pray also that the eyes of your heart may be enlightened in order that you may know the hope to which He has called you, the riches of His glorious inheritance in the saints, and His incomparably great power for us who believe" (Ephesians 1:16-19).

Paul prayed that the "eyes of their heart" would be enlightened, that they would be able to know God—and God's plans for them, and God's inheritance for them, and God's power for them—not just in their heads, but in their hearts.

It's a prayer that I know God answers because I've seen Him answer it in my own life, and because I've seen Him answer it when I've prayed it for others.

The most memorable time I watched God answer this prayer was when I was praying for a woman who was dying of cancer. She believed in her head that God loved her, but because her battle with cancer had taken up so much of her life, she had trouble believing it in her heart. I went to see her to pray for her healing, but when we finally sat down to pray, I asked her what she would like me to pray for her. She said simply that she'd like to hear God's voice, to hear him speak directly to her heart. She said she had been a Christian for so many years, yet she had never heard God speak to her personally.

It wasn't that she hadn't read the Bible, or hadn't been to church. She had done both all her life. It was just that she didn't feel that what she had read about God's love and grace applied to her *personally*.

All I could do at that point was to pray. To pray that God would open the eyes of her heart. To pray that God would speak to her in a way that she could understand it and believe it personally, not just in her head, but deep inside her heart. So we prayed, and I went back home.

I got a call from her a few days later. She told me that she was sicker than she had ever been in her life. But she went on to say that even though she felt sicker than ever before, she felt, for the first time in her life, that God had truly spoken to her. She could hardly describe it, but she said that she went to a special church service that weekend and the speaker was talking about God's lavish love from the book of Ephesians. And for the first time in her life, she felt that God was speaking those words directly to her.

In the weeks that followed, she and her husband took communion together every day, experiencing a sweet fellowship with each other and with the Lord until the day finally came that He took her home to commune with Him forever. God had answered her prayer.

If you'd like to experience God's love and grace in a personal way, not just in your head, but deep inside your heart, let me encourage you to pray. Pray that God would open the eyes of your heart, that you may know Him better. Let Him pour out His glorious and lavish grace on you today.

PRAYER: FATHER, THANK YOU FOR GIVING ME A GLIMPSE OF YOUR GLORIOUS AND LAVISH GRACE. THANK YOU FOR TELLING ME ABOUT IT THROUGH THE WORDS OF THE BIBLE AND THROUGH THE WORDS OF THOSE WHO HAVE EXPERIENCED IT THEMSELVES. I PRAY THAT YOU WOULD OPEN THE EYES OF MY HEART SO THAT I COULD KNOW YOU BETTER. HELP ME TO EXPERIENCE YOUR GLORIOUS AND LAVISH GRACE IN A FRESH WAY TODAY. IN JESUS' NAME, AMEN.

GOD'S GRACE
IS A GIFT

Scripture Reading: Ephesians 2:1-10

Have you ever been able to tell someone some good news? It feels great, doesn't it? I was able to be the bearer of good news to someone this week, and it was a lot of fun.

Someone had heard about our upcoming trip to Israel this fall and wanted to surprise one of the worship leaders at their church with a gift: an all-expense paid trip to come with us to Israel.

The donor of the trip wanted to remain anonymous and asked me to call the recipient to tell him about the gift. When I made the call, this worship leader was overcome to the point of tears, unable to believe what he was hearing. He had told me before that he desperately wanted to come with us, but it would take a miracle.

When I told him his miracle had just happened, he asked, "Are you sure they wanted to give it to *me?* I don't deserve it! How could I ever pay them back?"

I told him he didn't have to pay it back. It was a gift. He didn't even have to deserve it. All he had to do was to receive it. If he wanted to go, all he had to do was say, "Yes." Through tears, he said, "Yes, I want to go!" And now, he's on his way!

Moments like these help me to understand God's gift of grace a little better.

When God offered me the gift of grace, to forgive me of my sins and give me the gift of eternal life, my reaction was much like this worship leader's: "Are you sure He wants to give it to me? I don't deserve it! How could I ever pay Him back?"

But God's gift of grace was just that—a gift. I didn't have to pay it back. I didn't even have to deserve it. All I had to do was receive it. If I wanted to be forgiven, saved, born again and given a new life—both here on earth and in heaven forever—all I had to do was to receive it by faith. Through tears, I said, "Yes, Lord, I believe." And now, I'm on my way!

The Apostle Paul gave a beautiful description of how all of this works in his letter to the Ephesians. He wrote:

"As for you, you were dead in your transgressions and sins, in which you used to live when you followed the ways of this world and of the ruler of the kingdom of the air, the spirit who is now at work in those who are disobedient. All of us also lived among them at one time, gratifying the cravings of our sinful nature and following its desires and thoughts. Like the rest, we were by nature objects of wrath. But because of His great love for us, God, who is rich in mercy, made us alive with Christ even when we were dead in transgressions —it is by grace you have been saved. And God raised us up with Christ and seated us with Him in the heavenly realms in Christ Jesus, in order that in the coming ages He might show the incomparable riches of His grace, expressed in His kindness to us in Christ Jesus. For it is by grace you have been saved, through faith—and this not from yourselves, it is the gift of God—not by works, so that no one can boast. For we are God's workmanship, created in Christ Jesus to do good works, which God prepared in advance for us to do" (Ephesians 2:1-10).

Paul reminded the Ephesians—and us—that God's grace is a gift.

You may feel like you don't deserve it, that your sins have pulled you down too far to receive God's wonderful gift of grace. But that's exactly why God sent Jesus to earth—not to condemn you for your sins, but to free you from them, inviting you to live with Him forever.

If you've never received God's gift of eternal life, it can be yours today. When your faith touches God's grace, the transaction is complete. Eternal life becomes yours. It's a gift that really is meant for you.

PRAYER: FATHER, THANK YOU FOR LOVING ME EVEN THOUGH THERE ARE TIMES WHEN I'M SURE I'VE BEEN UNLOVABLE. I'M SORRY FOR THE THINGS I'VE DONE WRONG IN MY LIFE, AND I WANT TO THANK YOU FOR SENDING JESUS TO DIE IN MY PLACE. FILL ME WITH YOUR HOLY SPIRIT. AND HELP ME TO LIVE MY LIFE FOR YOU FROM THIS DAY FORWARD. IN JESUS' NAME. AMEN.

God's Grace Draws You Near

Scripture Reading: Ephesians 2:11-22

God's grace is like a powerful magnet: it draws you close to Him. No matter how far away you may feel from God, God can still draw you near.

There's an old joke that says that the Prime Minister of Israel came to visit the President of the United States in his office one day. The Prime Minister noticed a red telephone on the President's desk. When the Prime Minister asked about it, the President said, "Oh, that's my direct line to God."

After a few minutes, the Prime Minister asked if he could use the phone. The President said, "Sure, but don't talk too long, because it's pretty expensive from here."

A few months later, when the President of the United States went to visit the Prime Minister of Israel in *his* office, he noticed the Prime Minister had a red phone on *his* desk, too. When the President found out that the phone did the same thing as his phone back home, he asked the Prime Minister if he could use it for just a few minutes.

The Prime Minister said, "Sure, and you can talk as long as you want! From here it's a local call."

While God does seem to have a special place in His heart for Israel, the truth is that no matter where you live in the world, you can talk to God anytime, for as long as you want. Every call to God is a local call when you place that call through Jesus Christ.

As the Apostle Paul wrote in his letter to the Ephesians, Christ destroyed the dividing wall that once separated the Jews from the Gentiles (or "non-Jews"), as well as the wall that once separated all people from their Creator. Now anyone can come near to God through Christ. Paul said:

> *"Therefore, remember that formerly you who are Gentiles by birth...were separate from Christ, excluded from citizenship in Israel and foreigners to the covenants of the promise, without hope and without God in the world. But now in Christ Jesus you who once were far away have been brought near through the blood of Christ.*

"For He Himself is our peace, who has made the two one and has destroyed the barrier, the dividing wall of hostility.... He came and preached peace to you who were far away and peace to those who were near" (Ephesians 2:11a, 12-14, 17).

God's grace draws you near. It doesn't matter how close or how far away you may feel you are, His grace can draw you in.

The first time I went to Israel, I stayed with a Muslim family on the West Bank. They were incredibly gracious and treated me like a king.

But as I thought about how close they lived to the paths where Jesus once walked and ministered and died, I also thought about how far away they were from the peace that Christ offers to all who put their faith in Him.

Even though I lived over 6,000 miles away from this land where Christ called His home, God's grace was still powerful enough to reach out to me on the other side of the world and draw me close to Him. He's not far from any one of us. As Luke, the writer of the book of Acts, says:

"From one man He [God] made every nation of

men, that they should inhabit the whole earth; and He determined the times set for them and the exact places where they should live. God did this so that men would seek Him and perhaps reach out for Him and find Him, though He is not far from each one of us" (Acts 17:26-27).

God is not far from you today. It doesn't matter where you were born or where you live. What matters is that you keep putting your faith in Christ, realizing that it was God's grace, demonstrated in Christ, that destroyed the dividing wall of hostility between you and God.

Reach out today and give Him a call. And feel free to talk as long as you want! No matter where you are, it's always a local call.

PRAYER: FATHER, THANK YOU FOR SENDING JESUS TO BRIDGE THE GAP BETWEEN ME AND YOU, AND BETWEEN ME AND MY FELLOW BELIEVERS. LORD, I PRAY THAT I WOULD BE ABLE TO EXPERIENCE JUST HOW NEAR YOU ARE TO ME TODAY, SENSING YOUR PRESENCE AS CLOSE AS THE VERY AIR I BREATHE. LORD, HELP ME TO REACH OUT TO YOU TODAY. IN JESUS' NAME, AMEN.

Lesson 5

GRACE GROWS
BEST IN WINTER

Scripture Reading: Ephesians 3:1-13

When you're going through tough times, it can be hard to see God at work in your life. Sometimes you begin to question whether He's really paying attention to your prayers. Sometimes you begin to question if He's even there at all.

If you're going through a tough time in your life right now, I want to encourage you that God is hearing your prayers. He does care. And He really is there. You may even find that God is at work doing the most important work He's ever done in your life.

It was at such a time as this that Samuel Rutherford, a Scottish minister who was imprisoned for his faith back in the 1600's, wrote to a friend about a truth he had discovered during that extremely difficult time. He wrote:

"I see that grace groweth best in winter."

When I think of the people I know who are among the most gracious, I realize that they are often the people who have been through some of the hardest circumstances in life.

The Apostle Paul was one of those people. Even though he was frequently beaten, robbed, imprisoned and left for dead, Paul didn't let those things crush his spirit. Instead, he put his faith in Christ even more. The more he suffered, the more he seemed to grow in grace.

Listen to how Paul described himself, both in terms of his own feelings of brokenness, and the grace that God had given him in his life:

> *"Although I am less than the least of all God's people, this grace was given me: to preach to the Gentiles the unsearchable riches of Christ, and to make plain to everyone the administration of this mystery, which for ages past was kept hidden in God, who created all things" (Ephesians 3:8-9).*

Compare this description of himself with two other descriptions he gave in two of his other letters.

The author J.I. Packer notes that in Paul's first letter to the Corinthians, written about 54 AD, Paul referred to himself as "the least of the apostles" (1 Corinthians 15:9). By the time he wrote his letter to the Ephesians, about 7 years later in 61 AD, Paul called himself "the least of all God's people" (Ephesians 3:8). But by the time he wrote his letter to Timothy, about 4 years after that in 65 AD, Paul described himself as the "chief of all sinners" (1 Timothy 1:15).

As Paul continued to walk with God through all those years of suffering, he went from considering himself as the least of the apostles, to the least of all God's people, to the chief of all sinners. It seems that the closer he got to God, the more aware he became of his own sinfulness. No wonder his letters are so filled with grace, using the word "grace" over 80 times throughout his letters in the New Testament. He truly saw God's grace at work in his own life and wanted to extend that grace to all those around him.

Paul knew the secret of how to handle suffering: keep looking up. Keep trusting in God to work things out for His glory. Paul said as much to the Ephesians, encouraging them to keep coming to God freely and confidently, not being discouraged by Paul's own sufferings:

"In Him and through faith in Him we may approach God with freedom and confidence. I ask you, therefore, not to be discouraged because of my sufferings for you, which are your glory" (Ephesians 3:12-13).

Paul saw that his suffering was not in vain, but would serve God's purpose in the end. As he wrote in his letter to the Romans:

"And we know that in all things God works for the good of those who love Him, who have been called according to His purpose" (Romans 8:28).

Whatever you're facing today, keep putting your faith in Christ. Keep trusting Him that He will work all things for your good as you continue to love Him, no matter how hard it may seem at the time. Grace, it seems, truly does grow best in winter.

PRAYER: FATHER, THANK YOU FOR YOUR GRACE THAT YOU HAVE SHOWERED UPON ME, EVEN IN THE

DIFFICULT TIMES. I PRAY THAT YOU WOULD HELP ME TO SEE THAT YOU'RE STILL AT WORK IN MY LIFE, EVEN WHEN THINGS LOOK LIKE THEY'RE FALLING APART. HELP ME TO KEEP TURNING TO YOU DURING THIS TIME, GROWING CLOSER TO YOU AND GROWING DEEPER IN YOUR GRACE. IN JESUS' NAME, AMEN.

How Much Are You Worth?

Scripture Reading: Ephesians 3:14-19

How much do you think you're worth? It depends on who you ask, and what they're counting.

If you were to ask an accountant, you'd find out that your worth could be extremely low or extremely high, depending on your assets. Michael Jackson, who created some of the most memorable music in history, was once asked by a reporter: "How much do you think you're worth?" Jackson replied, "It's way up there." Michael was counting the value of his accumulated wealth, including his 50% ownership of the entire Beatles music collection.

If you were to ask *Wired* magazine, you'd find out that you're worth about $45 million. That's because they're counting the value of the organs, tissues, and fluids that make up your body, assuming it were legal to sell them on the open market (which it's not). According to hospital and insurance estimates, your bone marrow alone is worth about $23 million, based on 1,000 grams at $23,000 per gram. One lung would be worth $116,400, a kidney $91,400 and a heart $57,000.

If you were to ask the U.S. Bureau of Chemistry and Soils, you'd find out that your net worth is just under one dollar. That's because they're counting your worth in terms of the market value of the chemicals and minerals that make up your body, including 65% oxygen, 18% carbon, 10% hydrogen, 3% nitrogen, and trace quantities of silicon, copper, aluminum, arsenic and so on.

But if you were to ask God, the One who created you and loves you more than anyone else in the world, you'd get an answer that blows all the others away.

That's because God counts your worth in terms of how much He loves you. But calculating God's love for you is nearly impossible. The Apostle Paul tried to express how much God loved the people in Ephesus, but he knew they would hardly be able to comprehend it. So he got down on his knees and prayed that they would have the power to grasp just how much God loved them. Here's what he wrote:

> *"For this reason I kneel before the Father, from whom His whole family in heaven and on earth derives its name. I pray that out of His glorious riches He may strengthen you with power through His Spirit in your inner being, so that Christ may dwell in your hearts through faith. And I pray that you, being rooted and established in love, may have power, together with all the saints, to grasp how wide and long and high and deep is the love of Christ, and to know this love that surpasses knowledge—that you may be filled to the measure of all the fullness of God" (Ephesians 3:14-19).*

How much are you worth? If you were to calculate it according to God's love for you, you'd find out that the answer is much closer to Michael Jackson's than any other: "It's way up there!"

When God created you, and the world in which you live, He spared no expense, lavishing His love on you with all kinds of colors, flavors, sights, sounds, attractions and delights.

And when God saw that you were going

astray, He spared no expense to get you back, paying more to save you than just $1 dollar, or $1,000 dollars or $45 million dollars. He paid more than an arm and a leg. He even paid more than what many consider the ultimate price—giving up His life for you. He went even further than that, and sacrificed the life of His most beloved Son, Jesus Christ.

And when Jesus died for you, He didn't do it because He had to, He did it because He wanted to. He did it because He loves you, because He considers you to be His friend.

"Greater love has no one than this," Jesus said, *"than He lay down His life for His friends" (John 15:13).*

You're worth more to God than you might even be able to comprehend. But still I pray that God will give you the power today to grasp just how "wide and long and high and deep is the love of Christ" ... for you.

PRAYER: FATHER, I PRAY THAT YOU WOULD GIVE ME THE POWER TODAY TO GRASP HOW WIDE AND LONG AND HIGH AND DEEP IS THE LOVE OF CHRIST FOR ME. I PRAY THAT YOU WOULD HELP ME TO

GIVE UP MY SIMPLE THOUGHTS THAT MAYBE YOU DON'T LOVE ME BECAUSE OF WHAT I HAVE OR DON'T HAVE, OR WHAT OTHERS SAY OR DON'T SAY ABOUT MY WORTH, BUT TO REALIZE JUST HOW VAST AND COMPLEX AND ASTOUNDING IS YOUR LOVE FOR ME. I PRAY THAT YOU WOULD OVERWHELM ME WITH YOUR LOVE TODAY IN A WAY THAT I CAN SEE IT, SENSE IT, KNOW IT, AND BELIEVE IT, DEEP IN MY HEART. IN JESUS' NAME, AMEN.

How Much Can You Imagine?

Scripture Reading: Ephesians 3:20-21

Have you ever found yourself to be a little disappointed with God, wondering why He hasn't answered your prayers in the way you thought He might?

You may *want* to pray in faith, but you also want to pray realistically. So how can you pray in a way that expresses your faith and trust in God, without being disappointed if you don't see the answers in the way that you expected?

For me, I've found that even if I overreach in my prayers, asking and expecting more from God in the short run than He actually provides, I know that in the long run He can still answer my prayers in a way that goes beyond anything I could have asked or imagined.

Back when I used to work as a computer analyst for a large company, I heard a professional technology forecaster say that the trouble with technology forecasting is that people often vastly *overestimate* the short-term impact of new technologies, but vastly *underes-timate* their long-term impact.

My own experience with the Internet was a prime example. When I saw a demonstration of the very first web browser, Mosaic, the presenter pulled up a page on his computer with a picture of three doors on it. As he clicked on each door, it pulled up a web page from a computer in Germany, then a page from a computer in another country, and finally a page from a computer in a third country. Everyone in the room was amazed. I began to imagine all kinds of possibilities of what could be done with such an easy-to-use worldwide network.

Yet with all the potential I could see or imagine for the Internet on that day, it paled in comparison to what the Internet has become today. It actually took several years for my initially high, short-term expectations of the Internet to finally become a reality within our company. But I could never have imagined the long-term impact the Internet would have on my own life in the future, forming the foundation for the rest of my life's work and ministry.

I think the same applies to our expectations of God. There are times when we tend to overestimate how God will answer our prayers in the short-term. But we vastly underestimate how God will answer our prayers in the long-term. While we may be disappointed in the short-term answers to our prayers, the long-term answers often go way beyond all we could ask or imagine.

In reading through one of my prayer journals from a few years ago, I ran across some disappointing days when I was trying to figure out how to fund the renovations at our Clover Ranch retreat house. When a job opportunity came up, I decided to apply, take on a second job, and put all the money I made at that job into the repairs on the house. When that job fell through even before I got started, I was disappointed.

But within a few months, God brought someone who not only donated enough to put a new roof on the house, but to completely redo the bathroom, the kitchen, and replace all the windows! I wrote in my journal that it was "beyond what I could imagine." My disappointment with God in the short run was replaced by amazement with God in the long run.

The Apostle Paul said it like this:

"Now to Him who is able to do immeasurably more than all we ask or imagine, according to His power that is at work within us, to Him be glory in the church and in Christ Jesus throughout all generations, for ever and ever! Amen" (Ephesians 3:20-21).

The next time you set out to ask God for something, ask boldly. But remember what God told the prophet Isaiah:

"As the heavens are higher than the earth, so are My ways higher than your ways, and My thoughts than your thoughts" (Isaiah 55:9).

By doing so, you can pray in faith and pray realistically, trusting God to answer in His way and His timing—and believing that He can do "immeasurably more than all you could ask or imagine."

PRAYER: FATHER, THANK YOU FOR YOUR WORD, WHICH SAYS EVEN MORE THAN I WOULD EXPECT IT TO SAY. THANK YOU FOR YOUR GRACE AND MERCY THAT ALLOWS US TO COME BEFORE YOU WITH OUR

REQUESTS. AND LORD, INCREASE MY FAITH SO
THAT I CAN COME TO YOU WITH BOLDNESS AND
CONFIDENCE, TRUSTING THAT YOU CAN INDEED DO
MORE THAN ALL I COULD ASK OR IMAGINE. IN
JESUS' NAME, AMEN.

Lesson 8

Extend Grace To Your Fellow Believers

Scripture Reading: Ephesians 4:1-6

Have you ever known people who can show incredible grace to those they hardly know, but who seem to withhold that grace from their fellow believers? I heard a joke that directly illustrates this problem:

I was walking across a bridge one day, and I saw a man standing on the edge, about to jump off. So I ran over and said, "Stop! Don't do it!"
"Why shouldn't I?" he said.
I said, "Well, there's so much to live for!"
He said, "Like what?"
I said, "Well, are you religious or atheist?"
He said, "Religious."
I said, "Me too! Are you Christian or Buddhist?"
He said, "Christian."
I said, "Me too! Are you Catholic or Protestant?"
He said, "Protestant."

I said, "Me too! Are your Episcopalian or Baptist?"

He said, "Baptist!"

I said, "Wow! Me too! Are you Baptist Church of God or Baptist Church of the Lord?"

He said, "Baptist Church of God!"

I said, "Me too! Are your Original Baptist Church of God or are you Reformed Baptist Church of God?"

He said, "Reformed Baptist Church of God!"

I said, "Me too! Are you Reformed Baptist Church of God, Reformation of 1879, or Reformed Baptist Church of God, Reformation of 1915?"

He said, "Reformed Baptist Church of God, Reformation of 1915!"

I said, "Die, heretic scum!" and I pushed him off.

That joke was voted the best religious joke of all time in an online poll a few years ago, probably because it hits so close to home for so many people. Maybe you've seen it happen yourself, where people who are otherwise extremely close to each other in their thoughts and beliefs let something *comparatively* minor cause a sharp disagreement.

God reminds us in the book of Ephesians

that He's extended incredible grace to us all, and He wants us to extend that same grace to our fellow believers. The Apostle Paul wrote:

"As a prisoner for the Lord, then, I urge you to live a life worthy of the calling you have received. Be completely humble and gentle; be patient, bearing with one another in love. Make every effort to keep the unity of the Spirit through the bond of peace. There is one body and one Spirit—just as you were called to one hope when you were called— one Lord, one faith, one baptism; one God and Father of all, who is over all and through all and in all" (Ephesians 4:1-6).

Paul says something similar in his letter to the Galatians:

"Therefore, as we have opportunity, let us do good to all people, especially to those who belong to the family of believers" (Galatians 6:10).

I know of a man who built one of the largest churches in India. A friend who knew him said that one of the reasons for his success was that he never, ever spoke a negative word against anyone or any church who was working in that country in the name of Christ, even if he disagreed with their doctrine or approach. As a result of his true graciousness, he was able to build bridges with many people, expanding the kingdom of God at every turn.

Jesus alluded to the same idea one day when the Apostle John came to Him and said:

> *"Teacher, we saw a man driving out demons in Your name and we told him to stop, because he was not one of us."*
>
> *"Do not stop him," Jesus said. "No one who does a miracle in My name can in the next moment say anything bad about Me, for whoever is not against us is for us. I tell you the truth, anyone who gives you a cup of water in my name because you belong to Christ will certainly not lose his reward."*
> *(Mark 9:39-41).*

The next time you're tempted to push someone off the bridge who is otherwise extremely close to you in their thoughts and beliefs, don't do it! Extend to them the same grace that God has extended to you. Give them a cup of cold water, in Jesus' name, making every effort "to keep the unity of the Spirit through the bond of peace."

PRAYER: FATHER, THANK YOU FOR REMINDING ME TO SEEK UNITY WITH MY FELLOW BELIEVERS, RATHER THAN TRYING TO FIND FAULT WITH THEM. HELP ME TO BE TRULY GRACIOUS TODAY, AND TRULY FORGIVING, WHEN I RUN ACROSS THOSE WHO APPROACH THEIR FAITH AND LIFE DIFFERENT THAN I DO. HELP ME FOCUS ON OUR SHARED LOVE FOR YOU AND EXTEND THE SAME KIND OF GRACE TO THEM THAT YOU'VE EXTENDED TO ME. IN JESUS' NAME, AMEN.

Lesson 9

Use Your Gifts
To Serve Others

Scripture Reading: Ephesians 4:7-16

I once belonged to a church that had 3,500 ministers! That's a lot of ministers! But it wasn't because they had 3,500 people on staff. It was because they considered every member a minister. They expected and encouraged every member to minister to others, to serve others, with the particular gifts that God had given them.

That was the church where I finally decided to put my faith in Christ. It wasn't just because of the great sermons, or the powerful Sunday School lessons, which were important. It was also because of the various members who reached out to me, who invited me to Bible studies in their homes, who prayed for me, and who served me—ministered to me—in various other ways.

When the truth of God's love for me in Christ finally broke through to my heart and mind, I decided to devote the rest of my life to serving Him, too. That didn't mean that I went immediately into "professional" ministry. It meant that I had now become the three-thousand, five hundred and first minister at that church, using the gifts God had given me to minister to others.

This is how the Bible describes ministry. While there are certainly specific gifts—or "graces," as the Bible sometimes refers to them— that are given to some to preach or teach, to prophesy or evangelize, or to oversee the workings of the church, these gifts are simply a means to an end: to equip the rest of God's people for works of service.

Here's how the Apostle Paul puts it in Ephesians chapter 4:

> "But to each one of us grace has been given as Christ apportioned it.... It was He who gave some to be apostles, some to be prophets, some to be evangelists, and some to be pastors and teachers, to prepare God's people for works of service, so that the body of Christ may be built up until we all reach unity in the faith and in the knowledge of the Son of God and become mature, attaining to the whole measure of the fullness of Christ" (Ephesians 4:7, 11-13).

The Apostle Peter puts it like this, in 1 Peter chapter 4:

"Each one should use whatever gift he has received to serve others, faithfully administering God's grace in its various forms. If anyone speaks, he should do it as one speaking the very words of God. If anyone serves, he should do it with the strength God provides, so that in all things God may be praised through Jesus Christ" (1 Peter 4:10-11a).

When I first put my faith in Christ and received the gift of eternal life, I was surprised to find out that God still had more gifts to give me! I thought eternal life was enough! But it wasn't enough for God. He still had more He wanted to do in and through me, so He poured other gifts into my life, gifts that were not just for me, but to equip me to serve others.

If you've already received the gift of eternal life by putting your faith in Christ, God still has more He wants to do in and through you, too.

For some of you, God has called you, gifted you, and equipped you with the ability to teach, preach, evangelize, prophesy and oversee His work here on the earth. If so, God wants you—*He needs you*—to use those gifts to equip others, "to prepare God's people for works of service."

For some of you, God has called you, gifted you, and equipped you with gifts of faith, mercy, encouragement, serving, giving, leadership, administration—and the list goes on and on (just read Paul's letters to the Corinthians, chapters 12 and 13, or to the Romans, chapter 12, for more about spiritual gifts and how to use them). But all gifts are given for the same reason, "so that the body of Christ may be built up until we all reach unity in the faith and in the knowledge of the Son of God and become mature, attaining to the whole measure of the fullness of Christ."

Your church doesn't have just one minister, or two, or ten or twenty. Every member is a minister, when you use your gifts to serve others.

PRAYER: FATHER, THANK YOU FOR GIVING ME THE GIFT OF ETERNAL LIFE, AND THANK YOU FOR GOING FURTHER AND GIVING ME EVEN MORE GIFTS BEYOND THAT! HELP ME TO THINK OF WAYS TODAY TO USE THE GIFTS YOU'VE GIVEN ME TO SERVE

OTHERS. HELP ME TO NOT NEGLECT THOSE GIFTS, BUT TO PUT THEM INTO PRACTICE SO THEY CAN GROW BETTER AND STRONGER, NOT ONLY FOR MY SAKE, BUT FOR THOSE YOU WANT TO TOUCH THROUGH ME. IN JESUS' NAME, AMEN.

Forgive As Christ Has Forgiven You

Scripture Reading: Ephesians 4:17-32

One of the things I've noticed about gracious people is that they often have an incredible capacity to overlook the faults of others and focus on their strengths instead. I suppose it's the same way that God looks at us, even if we don't always perceive it that way.

While it might seem that gracious people could be simply unaware of just how sinful others can be, usually just the opposite is true. Gracious people, like God, often seem to understand sin and just how destructive sin can be. But just like God, they also understand something else. They understand just how powerful forgiveness can be.

As a result, when faced with a sin in someone else's life, those who are filled with grace make a conscious decision to choose forgiveness over anger, blessing over cursing, and compassion over destruction.

The Apostle Paul understood these choices as well. In his letter to the Ephesians, he urged them to give up their thoughts of anger, rage and malice, and to extend forgiveness, grace and kindness instead. He wrote:

" 'In your anger do not sin': Do not let the sun go down while you are still angry, and do not give the devil a foothold... Do not let any unwholesome talk come out of your mouths, but only what is helpful for building others up according to their needs, that it may benefit those who listen. And do not grieve the Holy Spirit of God, with whom you were sealed for the day of redemption. Get rid of all bitterness, rage and anger, brawling and slander, along with every form of malice. Be kind and compassionate to one another, forgiving each other, just as in Christ God forgave you" (Ephesians 4:26-27, 29-32).

Forgiveness is at the heart of grace. It's what makes Christ Himself so gracious. The Bible says that Christ didn't wait for us to turn from our sins before He was willing to die for us, but rather,

"While we were still sinners, Christ died for us" (Romans 5:8b).

That's grace. That's forgiveness. That's what God has done for us in Christ. And that's what God wants us to do for others.

Being gracious isn't about ignoring, or excusing, other people's sin. Being gracious is about forgiving other people's sin—because God, in Christ, has forgiven you of yours.

In Matthew 18, Jesus tells the parable of the unmerciful servant. In the story, Jesus tells about a king who forgives one of his servants of a huge debt. But when that servant goes home and demands repayment of a debt that one of his fellow men owed to him, the king had the unmerciful servant thrown into prison, saying that he wouldn't get out until he paid back all he owed. Jesus' ends the story with these words:

"This is how My heavenly Father will treat each of you unless you forgive your brother from your heart" (Matthew 18:35).

If someone has wronged you, God understands. He knows the hurt and pain that sin can cause. But He also knows how heavy it can be to carry around the burden of anger, as well as the burden of what's been done to you. You don't have to carry both. Let go of the anger, and let God heal the hurt.

When Jesus taught His disciples how to pray, he included these words: "Forgive us our debts, as we also have forgiven our debtors" (Matthew 6:12). Then He added these sobering words:

"For if you forgive men when they sin against you, your heavenly Father will also forgive you. But if you do not forgive men their sins, your Father will not forgive your sins" (Matthew 6:14-15).

If anyone understands forgiveness, it's Christ. And if anyone can help you to forgive others when they've sinned against you, it's Christ, too. Let Him help you to forgive. Let Him show you what true grace is about by teaching you how to extend it to others. Then one day, when others look to you and say, "How can you be so gracious!?!" you'll be able to say, "Because Christ has been so gracious to me."

PRAYER: OUR FATHER IN HEAVEN, HALLOWED BE YOUR NAME, YOUR KINGDOM COME, YOUR WILL BE DONE ON EARTH AS IT IS IN HEAVEN. GIVE US TODAY OUR DAILY BREAD. FORGIVE US OUR DEBTS, AS WE ALSO HAVE FORGIVEN OUR DEBTORS. AND LEAD US NOT INTO TEMPTATION, BUT DELIVER US FROM THE EVIL ONE, FOR YOURS IS THE KINGDOM AND THE POWER AND THE GLORY FOREVER. AMEN. (FROM MATTHEW 6:9-13)

Lesson 11

LIVE A LIFE
OF LOVE

Scripture Reading: Ephesians 5:1-18

I love the title of today's message: "Live A Life Of Love." That phrase is full of alliteration, ...all the "l's" and "v's" and "f's" combine to make it just roll off your lips: "Live A Life Of Love."

I remember back in college I thought I was doing just that. I thought I was living a life of love, enjoying my friendships to my heart's content, and loving others as best I knew how.

But when the pain of the inevitable broken relationships finally caught up with me, I realized that I wasn't really living a life of love. It was more like a life of lust, and for some reason, that phrase just doesn't have the same ring to it.

I found out why, a few years later, as I began to read the Bible for the first time as an adult. I finally saw that I had been crossing boundaries in my relationships that God never intended for me to cross. I began searching the Scriptures for everything else that God had to say about love and life and I was amazed at what I discovered.

As I stepped into God's plan for my life in this area, I found that His way of loving was way better than anything I had imagined. I was so thankful that I took the time to discover what He said about these things instead of just following my own plans.

So now, when I see others heading down the same path that I had been on, I want to warn them, encourage them, help them to get back onto God's path. I want to share with them the same things that the Apostle Paul shared with the Ephesians when he said:

> *"Be imitators of God, therefore, as dearly loved children and live a life of love, just as Christ loved us and gave Himself up for us as a fragrant offering and sacrifice to God. But among you there must not be even a hint of sexual immorality, or of any kind of impurity, or of greed, because these are improper for God's holy people. Nor should there be obscenity, foolish talk or coarse joking, which are out of place, but rather thanksgiving.... For it is shameful even to mention what the disobedient do in secret" (Ephesians 5:1-3).*

Paul encouraged the Ephesians to live a life of love, but to do so in a way that didn't have even a *hint* of sexual immorality. And God wants us to do the same.

I read this week about a governor who lived his life according to this approach...at least, most of the time. But once a year he'd take a trip with some friends to "let steam out of the box." Those annual outings eventually undid him. What started as seemingly innocent fun turned into sharing his email address with a stranger, then meeting up with her again in the future. It eventually turned into a full-blown affair—and a full-blown nightmare. The relationship resulted in the destruction of his marriage, his career, and his relationship with God.

While I know that God can still work in his life to sort things out, to bring some good out of all the bad that's been done, I also know that it didn't have to be this way. God wasn't trying to "box him in" by saying he shouldn't have even a hint of sexual immorality. God was trying to help him "live a life of love," one that would truly lead to the abundant life that God intends for you and me, too.

Maybe you're like me and you're wondering

if you may have crossed some lines that God never intended for you to cross. If so, I'd encourage you to take a close look at God's Word so you can find out for sure. As Paul said to the Ephesians:

"Live as children of light....and find out what pleases the Lord... Therefore do not be foolish, but understand what the Lord's will is" (Ephesians 5:8b, 10, 17).

Find out what pleases the Lord, and take time to understand what His will is. Then you'll truly be able to "live a life of love."

PRAYER: FATHER, THANK YOU FOR GIVING ME LIFE, AND THANK YOU FOR SHOWING ME HOW TO LIVE A LIFE OF LOVE—THROUGH CHRIST. I PRAY THAT YOU WOULD HELP ME TO GIVE MY LIFE TO OTHERS, JUST AS HE GAVE HIS LIFE FOR ME. LORD, HELP ME TO DROP ANYTHING IN MY LIFE THAT HAS EVEN A HINT OF SEXUAL IMMORALITY IN IT, AND HELP ME TO NEVER CROSS ANY BOUNDARIES THAT YOU DON'T WANT ME TO CROSS. IN JESUS' NAME, AMEN.

Lesson 12

LET YOUR HEART SING

Scripture Reading: Ephesians 5:19-20

When I think of gracious people, it seems like they're often walking around with a song in their hearts. Whether any songs actually come out of their mouths or not, it seems like their words are practically musical, as if they're flowing out from songs being sung deep within them.

The Apostle Paul encouraged the Ephesians speak to each other with songs, too. He wrote:

> *"Speak to one another with psalms, hymns and spiritual songs. Sing and make music in your heart to the Lord, always giving thanks to God the Father for everything, in the name of our Lord Jesus Christ" (Ephesians 5:19-20).*

There's something about singing that brings joy to the surface. And there's something about having a song in your heart that spreads joy to those around you.

I have a nine-year-old son who can sing about anything. He'll sing about brushing his teeth, or a bumblebee he just saw, or a trip he's about to take. Whatever the topic, he's glad to sing about it. Sometimes he doesn't even have words for his songs—he'll just start humming a tune as he's walking around or riding in a car, letting the music flow from within him.

What has struck me about his singing is that whenever he sings, he's happy. It's not like he's always happy before he starts singing. But once he starts, his whole outlook and disposition changes. The songs themselves seem to bring joy into his heart and life.

I decided to try it myself this week when I was riding with some of my kids in the car. Every once in awhile, I'd need to remind them to talk nicer to each other, or to act more sweetly. So I began singing my reminders to my kids rather than speaking. Even though I didn't have much of a tune to what I was singing, the words came out much more pleasant and brought more smiles. It's hard to be angry when you're singing! It was a good lesson for me.

And it was a good reminder of the power of these verses from Ephesians. If you can try to keep a song in your heart, giving thanks to the Lord for all things, you'll be more gracious, more cheerful, more helpful, and get a better response from those around you. It doesn't mean that you have to sing about everything that comes into your mind, or else the person at the drive-up window might start to wonder about you. But it might just bring a bigger smile to your face and the faces of those around you to *think* about singing whatever you're going to say, even if you don't actually sing it.

My family and I were in a nursing home this week visiting a close friend who's is in the final days of her life. Although she wasn't able to respond much, she seemed to perk up when we sang a song or two for her. We didn't sing any big or fancy songs, just some songs that we all happened to know and that we sometimes sing as prayers before we eat. Maybe you've heard of the "Johnny Appleseed" song or the "Superman" prayer. They're simple, but thankful songs.

Even though they were just simple songs, they seemed to lift the spirits of everyone in the room, even in the face of impending death. Songs have a way of helping us refocus our thoughts and reframing our situations, especially songs of thanks and praise to God.

If you need a lift in your spirit today, or want to give a lift to the spirits of those around you, try singing a song. Make some music in your heart and let it flow out of your mouth. Even if you don't feel much like singing, you may find that singing is exactly "the cure for what ails ya'."

If you need some ideas where to start, take a look at the book of Psalms, which means "songs." Try speaking or singing the words to one of the Psalms out loud. Then consider sharing those words with those around you, and see what a blessing it can be.

PRAYER: FATHER, THANK YOU FOR ENCOURAGING ME TO SING AND MAKE MUSIC IN MY HEART TO YOU. HELP ME TO SING TO YOU IN A WAY THAT BLESSES YOU, BLESSES THOSE AROUND ME, AND BLESSES MY OWN HEART AS WELL. LORD, FILL ME WITH YOUR SPIRIT AGAIN TODAY, THE SPIRIT THAT BRING MUSIC TO MY LIFE. IN JESUS' NAME, AMEN.

Lesson 13

SUBMIT TO ONE ANOTHER ~ PART 1

Scripture Reading: Ephesians 5:21-33

One of the hardest things to do in life is what Paul asked the Ephesians to do in Ephesians chapter 5. Paul wrote:

"Submit to one another out of reverence for Christ" (Ephesians 5:21).

It may not sound that hard. In fact, it probably sounds quite reasonable. It's like listening to Jesus, and nodding in agreement, when He says, "Love one another" (John 13:34). Of course we should love one another. That's the most reasonable thing in the world to do. But it took on a whole new meaning when Jesus defined what it meant to "love one another." Jesus said:

"Greater love has no one than this, that he lay down his life for his friends" (John 15:13).

When your life is at stake, it's no longer quite as simple or convenient to "love one another." It's especially hard when the other person you're supposed to be loving just happens to be a jerk. But Jesus went beyond just loving his friends. The Bible says that Jesus laid down His life even for those who were sinning against Him. Paul wrote:

> *"Now, most people would not be willing to die for an upright person, though someone might perhaps be willing to die for a person who is especially good. But God showed His great love for us by sending Christ to die for us while we were still sinners"* (Romans 5:7-8, NLT).

It's the same thing with submission. It might sound easy enough to "submit to one another." But the truth is, none of us want to submit to anyone! It goes against human nature. It goes against "free will." It goes against the "rugged individualism" that many people think made our country so great.

But by submitting to one another, by surrendering your will to someone else's, you're demonstrating your love to them in one of the greatest ways possible. While it may be one of the most difficult things to do in life, it's also one of the most gracious. And it can turn your relationships around in a heartbeat.

I got a call one night from a couple who was having a knockdown, drag-out fight. I had only recently met them, and the wife said she was trying to decide if she should call me or call the police. When I got to their door and heard them fighting inside, I was wondering myself if she should have called the police instead!

But when we all sat down to talk, it turned out that the husband truly loved his wife, and the wife truly loved her husband. But their lives were so busy that when the husband wanted to spend more time with his wife, he expressed it in anger and frustration at their schedule, and she gave it right back to him with frustrations of her own. It quickly became a battle of the wills, and the fighting escalated from there.

I asked the wife if she believed her husband truly loved her, and if she could see that his anger grew out of an honest desire to spend more time with her, and she said, "Yes." I asked the husband if his wife were in danger, would he willingly give up his life for her, and he said, "Yes."

Then I shared with them the next words that Paul wrote to the Ephesians:

"Wives, submit to your husbands as to the Lord....Husbands, love your wives, just as Christ loved the church and gave Himself up for her..." (Ephesians 5:22, 25).

That truth helped them through another night. I'm thankful to say it's now been over fifteen years since that night, and they're still together and serving the Lord. It's hard work to submitting to one another, surrendering your will to someone else's. But the benefits to you, to others, and to the Lord far outweigh the work involved.

Submit to one another out of reverence for Christ. Lay down your life for those you love —and even for those who are sinning against you. As you do, I pray that God's love and grace will flow from you to them—just as it flowed from Christ to you.

PRAYER: FATHER, THANK YOU FOR CHALLENGING ME TO SUBMIT TO ONE ANOTHER OUT OF

REVERENCE FOR YOUR SON. LORD, EVEN THOUGH I KNOW IT'S HARD, I PRAY THAT YOU WOULD GIVE ME YOUR SPIRIT TO HELP ME TO DO IT, FOR I WANT TO BE AS GRACIOUS AND LOVING AS I CAN BE, AND I WANT TO HONOR YOU IN ALL I DO. IN JESUS' NAME, AMEN.

Lesson 14

Submit To One Another ~ Part 2

Scripture Reading: Ephesians 6:1-4

When the Apostle Paul told the Ephesians to "submit to one another out of reverence for Christ," he followed it up with several practical examples for how to do this in real life. In chapter 6, Paul described how children and parents can "submit to one another":

> *"Children, obey your parents in the Lord, for this is right. 'Honor your father and mother'—which is the first commandment with a promise—'that it may go well with you and that you may enjoy long life on the earth.'*
> *"Fathers, do not exasperate your children; instead, bring them up in the training and instruction of the Lord" (Ephesians 6:1-3).*

It's hard being a parent. But it's hard being a child, too.

Maybe you heard about the man who observed a woman in the grocery store with a three-year-old girl in her basket. As they passed the cookie section, the little girl asked for cookies and her mother told her, "No." The little girl immediately began to whine and fuss, and the mother said quietly, "Now Jane, we just have half of the aisles left to go through—don't be upset. It won't be long now."

Soon, they came to the candy aisle and the little girl began to shout for candy. When told she couldn't have any, she began to cry. The mother said, "There, there, Jane, don't cry—only two more aisles to go and then we'll be checking out."

When they got to the checkout stand, the little girl immediately began to clamor for gum and burst into a terrible tantrum upon discovering there'd be no gum purchased. The mother said serenely, "Jane, we'll be through this check out stand in 5 minutes and then you can go home and have a nice nap."

The man followed them out to the parking lot and stopped the woman to compliment her. "I couldn't help noticing how patient you were with little Jane. It's quite commendable," he remarked.

The mother replied, "I'm Jane. My little girl's name is Tammy."

It takes a lot of patience to be gracious, especially between children and parents. Yet Paul tells us there's value in doing so.

For children, Paul points out that obeying your parents is the first of the Ten Commandments with a promise: "that it may go well with you and enjoy a long life on the earth." Not only do things go better for you, but children someday may grow up to have children of their own and realize that "what goes around comes around." I've heard it said that "diaper" spelled backwards is "re-paid!"

For parents, Paul says not to exasperate your children, meaning not to irritate them so much that that they become enraged. "Instead," Paul says, "bring them up in the training and instruction of the Lord." King Solomon knew the long-term benefits of training a child in how to live a godly life. He said:

"Train a child in the way he should go, and when he is old he will not turn from it" (Proverbs 22:6).

And some of you may find yourself in the

same place that my wife and I are in right now: taking care of both your children and your parents at the same time, as Lana's parents have moved in with us as their health has started to decline. Even after all these years as children and as parents, we're still in the process of learning what it means to "obey your parents in the Lord," and to "not exasperate your children."

Some days it means holding your tongue when you'd rather talk back. Other days it means speaking the truth in love when you'd rather not talk at all. At times it means serving a meal and cutting up someone's food. At other times, it means training someone else how to make a serve a meal and cut up their own food. Quite often it means surrendering your will to accommodate someone else's. But occasionally it means exerting your own will for the benefit of everyone involved.

Submit to one another out of reverence to Christ. You'll be blessed—and so will those around you—when you do.

PRAYER: FATHER, THANK YOU FOR REMINDING ME TO HOW TO SUBMIT TO ONE ANOTHER OUT OF REVERENCE FOR CHRIST, ESPECIALLY TO THOSE

CLOSEST TO ME. HELP ME TO KNOW HOW TO APPLY THESE WORDS IN PRACTICAL WAY TODAY, WHETHER THAT'S HONORING MY PARENTS AND OR TRAINING MY CHILDREN IN YOUR WAYS, OR BOTH. LORD, HELP ME TO DO THESE THINGS IN A WAY THAT BLESSES YOU, BLESSES THEM, AND BLESSES ME AS WELL. IN JESUS' NAME, AMEN.

SUBMIT TO ONE
ANOTHER ~ PART 3

Scripture Reading: Ephesians 6:5-9

When Paul encouraged the Ephesians to "submit to one another out of reverence for Christ" (Ephesians 5:21), he gave them three practical examples for how to do this: one for husbands and wives, one for parent and children, and one for masters and slaves.

While the terms "masters" and "slaves" may not apply to many people today, the terms "employers" and "employees" certainly do. And Paul's words to the Ephesians are just as fitting for these types of working relationships, too. Listen to Paul's words, and see how they might apply to you today:

"Slaves, obey your earthly masters with respect and fear, and with sincerity of heart, just as you would obey Christ. Obey them not only to win their favor when their eye is on you, but like slaves of Christ, doing the will of God from your heart. Serve

wholeheartedly, as if you were serving the Lord, not men, because you know that the Lord will reward everyone for whatever good he does, whether he is slave or free.

"And masters, treat your slaves in the same way. Do not threaten them, since you know that He who is both their Master and yours is in heaven, and there is no favoritism with Him" (Ephesians 6:5-9).

I don't know about you, but I've had a fair share of bosses in my lifetime. Some of which I had great respect for, and others of which I had very little respect for. But as I look at Paul's words, he never said anything about whether or not a master was worthy of respect, but that we were to treat them with respect, obeying them just as we would obey Christ.

I know from experience just how hard that can be. But I also know from experience just how beneficial that can be, often doing more for my working relationships than I could have imagined.

In one instance, I had a boss who didn't like me from day one—and he let me know it. He had heard I was some kind of go-getter and he wasn't about to let me go anywhere. Things went from bad to worse.

One day he asked me to do yet one more thing that I felt was about to push me over the edge. It wasn't immoral or unethical—he simply asked me to fill out a survey that the company had distributed, asking employees to fill it out voluntarily and anonymously. But since I was out of town when the survey was distributed, he sent me a copy and told me I had to fill mine out and fax it back to him by the following day.

I took issue with his request, since it was supposed to be voluntary and anonymous. By mandating that I fill it out, and then fax it back with my phone number right there on the fax, it would violate both of those conditions.

But after making my case, he still held onto his position, and I held onto mine. Late that night, Paul's words to the Ephesians came back to me, to "obey your earthly masters with respect and fear...just as you would obey Christ." Even though I disagreed with his approach, I filled out the survey and faxed it back to him so it would be on his desk in the morning.

Our whole relationship turned around that day. My boss became my biggest champion from that day forward and for the rest of my career at that company. It was a lesson that proved once more than God's words spoken through Paul were true, that God really will "reward everyone for whatever good he does." And it was a lesson that helped me when I later became an employer myself—and a husband and a father.

Submitting to one another really does work! It demonstrates a graciousness on your part, and can make your relationships flow better all around—whether they're between husbands and wives, parents and children, or "masters and slaves." Don't miss out on the reward God has for you! Submit to one another out of reverence for Christ!

PRAYER: FATHER, THANKS FOR THE REMINDER TO SUBMIT TO TO THOSE WITH WHOM I WORK, WHETHER I WORK FOR THEM OR THEY WORK FOR ME. HELP ME TO BE GRACIOUS IN MY RELATIONSHIPS WITH EACH PERSON IN THE WORKPLACE, SO THAT YOUR BLESSINGS WOULD FLOW TO US AND THROUGH US. HELP ME IN ALL MY

RELATIONSHIPS TO SUBMIT TO ONE ANOTHER OUT OF REVERENCE TO CHRIST. IN JESUS' NAME, AMEN.

Lesson 16

OVERCOME YOUR
ENEMIES WITH GRACE

Scripture Reading: Ephesians 6:10-18

One of the best ways to overcome your enemies is to make them your friends.

I made a friend like this back in college. When we were taking an English Literature class together, it seemed like we were always at odds. I was always defending King Arthur as the hero of the books, and she was always defending Queen Guinevere. In class, it seemed like we'd never agree on anything.

But one day we both showed up for tryouts at a college musical. We realized we had more in common than we thought, and both of us softened up in our approach. That softening had such an effect on our friendship, that a few years after college was over, she even agreed to sing at my wedding.

There are times when God calls you to overcome your enemies by destroying them so completely that they no longer have an effect on your life. But there are other times when God calls you to overcome your enemies by winning them over with your love, realizing that the battle may not be against them, but against spiritual forces that may be turning them against you.

The Apostle Paul talks about these battles in his letter to the Ephesians, and the kinds of weapons that God gave them to fight these battles. You might call these "weapons of grace," weapons that can turn your enemies into your friends!

Listen to these words as Paul describes this spiritual "armor of God."

"Finally, be strong in the Lord and in His mighty power. Put on the full armor of God so that you can take your stand against the devil's schemes. For our struggle is not against flesh and blood, but against the rulers, against the authorities, against the powers of this dark world and against the spiritual forces of evil in the heavenly realms. Therefore put on the full armor of God, so that when the day of evil comes, you may be able to stand your ground, and after you have done everything, to stand. Stand firm then, with the belt of truth buckled around your waist, with the

breastplate of righteousness in place, and with your feet fitted with the readiness that comes from the gospel of peace. In addition to all this, take up the shield of faith, with which you can extinguish all the flaming arrows of the evil one. Take the helmet of salvation and the sword of the Spirit, which is the Word of God. And pray in the Spirit on all occasions with all kinds of prayers and requests. With this in mind, be alert and always keep on praying for all the saints" (Ephesians 6:10-18).

The next time someone comes against you, speaks against you, or tries to overpower you, go ahead and put on your battle gear. But instead of gearing up with all your usual defenses, try some of God's. To paraphrase the Apostle Paul:

Be truthful. Be righteous. Be eager to share the gospel of peace. Keep up your faith. Keep in mind that Jesus has already saved you. Speak the truth in love. And keep on praying, continually.

These are God's weapons of grace, weapons that you can use to defend yourselves, and disarm your opponents, oftentimes with a greater impact than physical weapons could have.

It was through Jesus' love and grace that He turned you from being His enemy to being His friend (see Romans 5:10 and John 15:15). So it shouldn't be surprising that God wants you to use these same weapons to overcome your enemies, making them your friends as well. It may not happen overnight, but over time you may just find their hearts softening towards you, as the real enemy, the power of darkness, has to flee when the light turns on.

Remember that your battle is not against flesh and blood, but against spiritual forces in the heavenly realm. In a spiritual battle, you need spiritual armor, which is much softer and more gracious than physical armor, but in the end, is much stronger and more powerful.

Put on your spiritual armor today. Clothe yourself with truth, righteousness, peace, faith, salvation, God's Word and prayer. Let God's love flow through you to those around you and watch what happens.

PRAYER: FATHER, THANK YOU FOR REMINDING ME THAT THE BATTLES I FACE AREN'T ALWAYS AGAINST AN ENEMY I CAN SEE, BUT AGAINST SPIRITUAL

FORCES IN THE HEAVENLY REALM. HELP ME TO PUT
ON MY SPIRITUAL ARMOR OF LOVE AND GRACE
TODAY SO THAT I CAN OVERCOME THOSE WHO ARE
AGAINST ME—AND EVEN MAKE THEM MY FRIENDS.
IN JESUS' NAME, AMEN.

Lesson 17

GRACE IS
"OTHERS-FOCUSED"

Scripture Reading: Ephesians 6:19-22

I'm sitting today with one of the most gracious women I know. It's not my wife, although she's quite gracious. And it's not anyone particularly famous, except to her family and to those of us who know her well.

Her name is Mary Lou Schrock, and she was a lifetime friend of my Dad's until he passed away earlier this year. She stepped back into his life about nineteen years ago, filling a void that was left after my mom passed away. Mary Lou has been like a second mother to me, coming to our kids' birthday parties, spending countless hours with my Dad during days of sickness and health, and spending Christmas mornings with our family year after year.

She's invested her life in taking care of others. But in recent years, she's had to let others take care of her. If she had a choice, I'm sure she'd gladly switch roles. That's just the kind of woman she is. And that's one of the things that makes her so gracious as well. Whether she was baking a meal for someone, or helping out at the nursing home, or writing a card to send to someone who needed a lift, she was always thinking of others.

In a way, she was very much like the Apostle Paul, who displayed a similar quality of graciousness. From the beginning of his letter to the Ephesians until the very end, he was always "others-focused." I can't imagine it was easy, though.

As a prisoner in Rome, I'm sure he could have written thousands of words talking about himself, complaining of the false accusations made against him, the unjust beatings he'd had to endure, or the hardships of life as a prisoner in the first century A.D. But instead, he wrote thousands of words talking about *them*, focusing on *their* lives, *their* trials, and *their* relationships with God.

The only time he asked for anything for himself was at the very end of his letter. And even then, his only request was for them to pray that he would be able to fearlessly proclaim the message of Christ to others, the very thing that landed him in prison in the first place. He wrote:

"Pray also for me, that whenever I open my mouth, words may be given me so that I will fearlessly make known the mystery of the gospel, for which I am in chains. Pray that I may declare it fearlessly, as I should" (Ephesians 6:19-20).

Paul was already on trial for proclaiming the good news about Jesus Christ, and he was awaiting a very likely death sentence for it. Yet he called on the Ephesians to pray that God would help him to keep proclaiming the message of Christ without fear. To the end, Even when asking for prayer for himself, Paul remained steadfastly committed to others. And God wants us to remain "others-focused" as well.

This doesn't mean that you can't talk about yourself, your problems and your needs. But it does mean that you should be thoughtful about when and how you share those needs. You don't want to be like the woman who said: "Enough about me. Let's talk about you. What do *you* think about me?"

As "others-focused" as he was, Paul knew

that it was also important to let others know how he was doing, too. So at the end of his letter, he wrote:

> *"Tychicus, the dear brother and faithful servant in the Lord, will tell you everything, so that you also may know how I am and what I am doing. I am sending him to you for this very purpose, that you may know how we are, and that he may encourage you"* (Ephesians 6:21-22).

Paul didn't ignore himself and his needs completely. But he was gracious enough to know there was an appropriate time and place to share those needs. And God wants us to do the same.

God wants us to be people who are "others-focused" to the core, people who regularly spend time thinking about the needs of others and how to meet those needs. He wants us to be people like Mary Lou, people who invest their lives in ways that will bless those around us.

PRAYER: FATHER, THANK YOU FOR HELPING ME SEE THAT GRACE IS "OTHERS-FOCUSED." I PRAY THAT YOU WOULD HELP ME TO BE SO FOCUSED ON

OTHERS THAT MY LIFE AND MY PROBLEMS WILL FADE
IN COMPARISON. HELP ME TO BE FILLED WITH
YOUR GRACE TO SUCH AN EXTENT THAT I WOULD
GLADLY POUR IT OUT ON OTHERS, REGARDLESS OF
THE COST TO ME PERSONALLY. LET ME BE A GOOD
AMBASSADOR FOR YOU, AND A GOOD MESSENGER OF
YOUR GRACE TO THOSE AROUND ME. IN JESUS'
NAME, AMEN.

How Gracious Is Gracious Enough?

Scripture Reading: Ephesians 6:23-24

As we come to the closing words of Paul's letter to the Ephesians, I'd like to touch on the idea of just how gracious we have to be in order to be "gracious enough." Just how much grace has God shown to us? And how much grace does He want us to show to others?

One of my favorite quotes on this topic goes like this:

> *"Sometimes you have to be overly gracious in order to be gracious enough."*

When I think of that quote, I think of a woman named Jean. Jean is a business woman from England whom we met on a missions trip a few years ago. She helped us out shortly after that trip by coming to a retreat center we're renovating here in Illinois called

Clover Ranch. She came to help us with some interior decorating.

But when she arrived, it became clear that the house needed much more than a coat of paint and some pretty pictures. While she was taking a bath one day, the pipes burst in the upstairs bathroom, pouring water down into the kitchen below. While replacing those pipes, it became clear that the wiring had to be redone as well. We ended up gutting both the bathroom and the kitchen entirely, starting again from scratch. Then the rain came and we realized that water was coming in around many of the old windows and they would have to be replaced before we could even think about any interior decorating. The house was a mess and she hadn't even gotten to start on what she initially came to do.

In spite of all of this, Jean was a trooper. We invited her to stay in our own home during all of this, but like the loyal captain of a ship, she wanted to stay with her vessel. She continued to live at Clover Ranch, without a functional kitchen or bathroom, except for a sink and a shower stall in the basement, and accompanied by a host of crickets and spiders and other creatures that seemed to thrive in the chaos of the reconstruction.

Through it all, Jean was not just gracious. She was *overly gracious*. She talked about how thankful she was to be out in the country, to have time to think and pray, and to be part of helping us out with this project.

While Lana and I felt bad that she had to live in such an inhospitable situation, Jean's grace helped ease our burden. She expressed over and over that she truly wanted to help us out. The only reason we could even possibly believe her was that she was consistently overly gracious. If she had just said, "It's OK, don't worry about it," that would have been gracious. But we would have still felt miserable for what was happening. Yet because of her overflowing graciousness, we were finally able to believe that she was sincere in her thankfulness and solid in her belief that God had placed her right where He wanted her to be for that season of her life.

Through her words and actions, Jean taught us the value of being overly gracious. Just saying a kind word or two doesn't always get the message across. Sometimes we need to be overly gracious, as God has been with us, in order for others to truly believe that we're sincere.

Like the Apostle Paul, who used the word *grace* a dozen times in his letter to the Ephesians, and another seventy-five times in his other letters in the New Testament, it may seem like we would never be able to talk about grace enough, to demonstrate it enough, to live it enough, or to truly express it enough so that others would be able to believe it and receive it.

But if we keep trying, if we keep sharing, if we keep expressing God's grace to others as if *God Himself* was expressing *His grace through us,* then perhaps others would begin to believe us. Just maybe they'd begin to realize how much we love them, and how much God loves them. Just maybe, by being "overly gracious," we'd finally be able to be "gracious enough."

PRAYER: FATHER, THANK YOU FOR BEING OVERLY GRACIOUS WITH ME. THANK YOU FOR EXPRESSING YOUR GRACE TO ME IN A WAY THAT I COULD BELIEVE IT AND RECEIVE IT. NOW, LORD, HELP ME TO DO THE SAME IN SHARING YOUR GRACE WITH OTHERS. IN JESUS' NAME, AMEN.

Conclusion

HAVING A
GRACE-FILLED HEART

Scripture Reading: Ephesians 6:24

As I was writing these messages about grace, someone asked me if I had any ideas for how they could have a more grace-filled heart—a heart that would help them to appreciate others more instead of complaining, to forgive instead of holding grudges, and to love instead of being angry.

Here's a summary of what I shared in response, taken from things I've learned from the book of Ephesians and other places in the Bible. I thought you might like to read them, too, as a summary of our study together:

1) Practice continual forgiveness. Forgiveness is the heart of the gospel, as Jesus forgave us even while we were still sinning against Him. It's the heart of showing grace towards others as well. As Paul said, "Be kind and compassionate to one another, forgiving each other, just as in Christ God forgave you"

(Ephesians 4:32). By choosing to forgive others, as God has forgiven you, you'll be well on your way towards having a grace-filled heart.

2) Fill your mind with the things of God. Paul wrote to the Philippians: "...whatever is true, whatever is noble, whatever is right, whatever is pure, whatever is lovely, whatever is admirable—if anything is excellent or praiseworthy—think about such things" (Philippians 4:8). By reading God's Word daily, memorizing verses of scripture, and meditating on what you're reading,you'll find that God will begin to fill your mind with His thoughts, His ideas and His point of view on whatever you're facing. Keep filling your heart and mind with the things of God as much as possible, every day, several times throughout the day. This will pay off with huge dividends for you and for those around you, both in the short-term and in the long-term.

3) Keep asking yourself, "What Would Jesus Do?" (WWJD). This is a simple, but helpful reminder to try to think and act and speak as Jesus would. It's not just an intellectual ex-

ercise. It's a practical way to accomplish God's work here on the earth. When Jesus went back to heaven, He sent His Holy Spirit to live inside us so that we could be His body—His hands, His feet, His eyes and ears and voice to those around us. Paul wrote to the Corinthians, "Now you are the body of Christ, and each one of you is a part of it" (1 Corinthians 12:27). As a believer in Christ, God wants to work through *you* as if Jesus Himself were doing the work—because He is!

4) Pray at all times. As Paul said to the Ephesians: "And pray in the Spirit on all occasions with all kinds of prayers and requests" (Ephesians 6:18). By praying throughout the day, seeking His will and listening for His voice, you'll be able to stay focused on what God wants at all times. It's like walking through the day with a friend—and even better—because Jesus is a friend who knows everything! So as you walk or sit or talk or think, keep on praying and talking to God at all times. It'll be both a joy to you and a practical help to those around you.

5) "Be quick to listen, slow to speak and

slow to become angry" (James 1:19). This practical reminder from James will help you you to spiritually "count to 10" before responding to others. While it doesn't say you can't get angry, or you can't ever say anything with which others might disagree, it does say to wait to speak until after you have listened carefully—meaning "with care" and "fully." When you do this, your words will simply come out better, expressing more love and grace, even when speaking things that may be hard to hear.

While having a grace-filled heart can take a lifetime, the Bible is full of practical steps that you can take right now to have an impact right away. That's the beauty of God's Word! It starts working as soon as you apply it to your life, and it keeps on working to the end. Put it into practice today, and may God fill you with His grace as you do.

As Paul said in his closing line to the Ephesians:

"Grace to all who love our Lord Jesus Christ with an undying love" (Ephesians 6:24).

PRAYER: FATHER, THANK YOU FOR THIS STUDY OF PAUL'S LETTER TO THE EPHESIANS. THANK YOU FOR THE WISDOM THAT YOU POURED INTO HIM, AND THANK YOU FOR PRESERVING THAT WISDOM IN THIS LETTER SO THAT WE CAN LEARN FROM IT EVEN 2,000 YEARS LATER. CONTINUE TO GIVE US A DESIRE TO LEARN ALL WE CAN FROM YOUR WORD, SO THAT WE CAN FILL OUR HEARTS WITH YOUR GRACE, AND THEN SHARE IT WITH OTHERS. IN JESUS' NAME, AMEN.

ABOUT THE AUTHOR

Described by *USA Today* as "a new breed of evangelist," Eric Elder is an ordained pastor and the creator of *The Ranch,* a faith-boosting website that attracts thousands of visitors each month at WWW.THERANCH.ORG.

Eric is also an author and speaker, having written about God for publications like Billy Graham's *Decision Magazine,* and spoken about faith at national conferences like the Exodus International *Freedom Conference.*

If you've enjoyed this book, you may enjoy some of Eric's other writings, including:

Two Weeks With God
Exodus: Lessons In Freedom
Jesus: Lessons In Love
Acts: Lessons In Faith
Nehemiah: Lessons In Rebuilding
and *What God Says About Sex*

To read, download or order more inspiring resources like this, please visit:

WWW.THERANCH.ORG